MEXICAN INDEPENDENCE DAY AND CINCO DE MAYO

REVISED AND UPDATED

Dianne M. MacMillan

Enslow Elementary

an imprint of

Enslow Publishers, Inc.

40 Industrial Road
Box 398
Berkeley Heights, NJ 07922
USA

http://www.enslow.com

Library of Congress Cataloging-in-Publication Data

MacMillan, Dianne M., 1943–

    Mexican Independence Day and Cinco de Mayo / Dianne M. MacMillan. — 2nd ed., rev. and updated.

        p. cm. — (Best holiday books)

    Summary: "Read about the beginning of Mexican Independence Day and Cinco de Mayo and see how these holidays are celebrated in the United States"—Provided by publisher.

    Includes bibliographical references and index.

    ISBN-13: 978-0-7660-3044-2

    ISBN-10: 0-7660-3044-X

    1. Mexico—Social life and customs—Juvenile literature. 2. Independence Day (Mexico)—History—Juvenile literature. 3. Cinco de Mayo (Mexican holiday)—History—Juvenile literature. 4. Cinco de Mayo, Battle of, Puebla, Mexico, 1862—Juvenile literature. 5. Juárez, Benito, 1806–1872—Juvenile literature. I. Title.

    F1210.M23 2008

    972—dc22

                                    2007002424

Printed in the United States of America

10 9 8 7 6 5 4 3 2 1

Illustration Credits: Alfred Wekelo/Shutterstock, p. 21; Associated Press, pp. 1, 6, 37, 40, 41, 43 (right); Colman Lerner Gerardo/Shutterstock, p. 13; Gail Williams, p. 4; Geoffrey Kuchera/Shutterstock, p. 7; The Granger Collection, New York, pp. 11, 14, 33; The Image Works, p. 44; iStockphoto, p. 35; Joseph McCullar/Shutterstock, p. 38; © 2007 Jupiter Corporation, pp. 8, 10, 12, 17, 28; Library of Congress, pp. 26, 27, 30, 32 (both); Marcuse, p. 19; Museum of Mexico City, p. 16; Neil Phillip Mey/Shutterstock, p. 31; Shutterstock, pp. 3, 23, 24, 36, 42; Steve Snowden/Shutterstock, p. 43 (left); Timothy Lee Lantgen/Shutterstock, p. 22.

Cover Photo: Associated Press

Contents

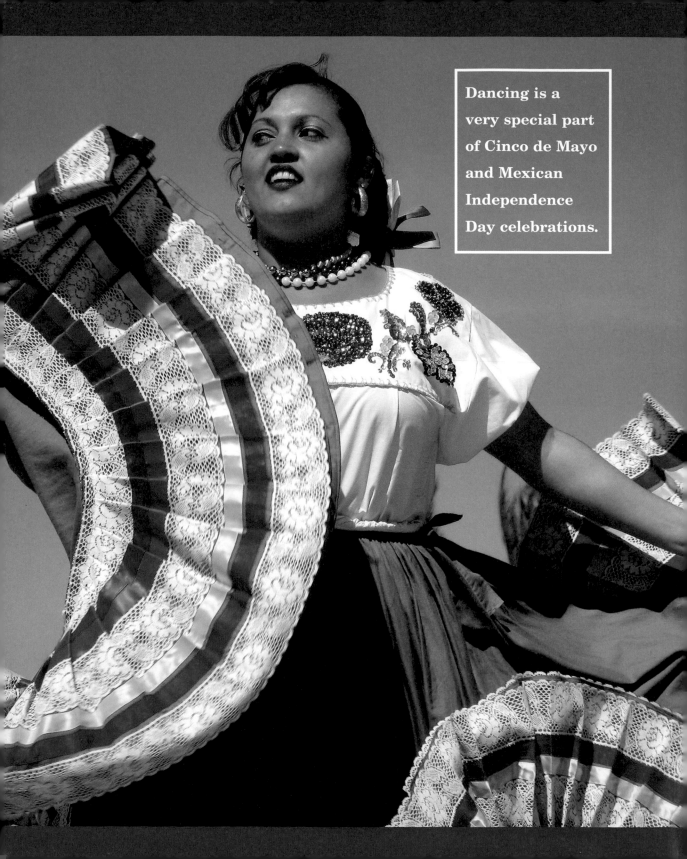

Dancing is a very special part of Cinco de Mayo and Mexican Independence Day celebrations.

OLÉ!

BOYS AND GIRLS SCREAM WITH DELIGHT AS they zoom down the high hill of a roller coaster. Ferris wheels turn round and round. On a stage, a group of children are dancing. The girls wear red and green full skirts. The boys have on white cotton pants and large white shirts. Red sashes are tied around their waists. On their heads are wide-brimmed hats called sombreros (som-BRAIR-os). The children twirl and stomp their feet.

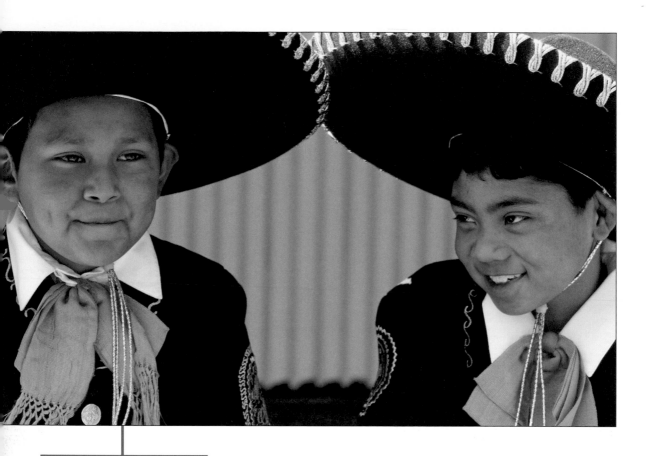

These boys are waiting to march in New York City's 2007 Cinco de Mayo parade.

Thousands of people have come together. There is music, talking, and laughter. Teenagers walk by, eating long, sugar-coated churros (CHOOR-ros). A band is playing and singing. Many people sing along. The sidewalk is lined with decorated booths. People sell hats, shawls called serapes (suh-RAH-pays), and baskets. There are also food booths. Delicious smells of tacos (TAH-kos), burritos (boor-REE-tos), and enchiladas (en-chuh-LAH-dahs) fill the air. They are made from thin, pancake-like pieces of bread folded around beans, meat and cheese. Children line up to buy Mexican pastries and cookies. These people are celebrating an important Mexican holiday.

Colorful serapes are pretty—and warm!

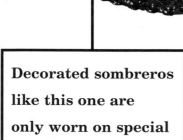

Decorated sombreros like this one are only worn on special occasions.

Families have come together to celebrate. All of this excitement is part of Mexican Independence Day. In many ways, it is like the Fourth of July in the United States.

Mexican Independence Day is celebrated on September 16. The date in Spanish is diez y seis de Septiembre (dee-es ee SAYS day sep-ti-EM-bray). It is an important day for Mexican Americans. In the spring on the fifth day of May, cinco de Mayo (SIN-coh day MY-oh), another celebration takes place. Cinco de Mayo remembers a special day in Mexican history.

These two days bring Mexican-American families together. They are proud of their history. Let's find out more about these holidays.

MEXICO

*

MANY MEXICAN AMERICANS WERE BORN IN Mexico. The country of Mexico is south of the United States. At one time, much of the land in the southwestern part of the United States belonged to Mexico.

Thousands of years ago, many different groups of native peoples lived in Mexico. Some of the largest groups were the Mayas (MAH-yahs), Toltecas (tol-TEC-ahs), Zapotecas (zah-po-TAY-cahs), and Aztecs (AZ-teks). They lived in large cities.

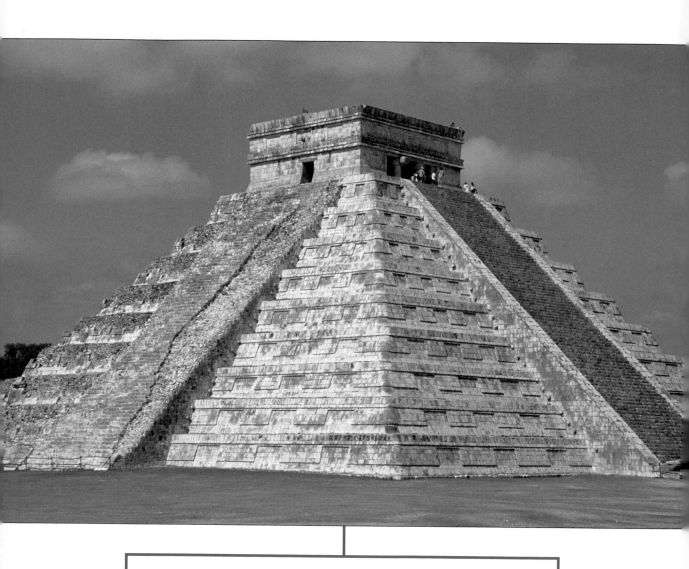

This pyramid in Mexico was built by the Mayans. It is often called El Castillo, or "the castle."

The cities had beautiful artwork and buildings. The Mayas and Aztecs built pyramids using stones.

In 1521, soldiers from Spain came to the New World. They conquered the people of Mexico. All of the land became a Spanish colony. The Spanish called the colony New Spain.

The Spaniards ordered the people of Mexico to speak Spanish. Spanish priests taught them Christian beliefs. A priest is a leader in the Catholic Church. For three hundred years, the country was under Spanish rule. Everything made or produced went to the king of Spain.

The Mexican people were not allowed to govern themselves except in their small towns. Many could not carry guns or

This painting shows the arrival of the Spanish. It was drawn by one of the Aztecs.

This map shows the part of Mexico that was a Spanish colony in 1610.

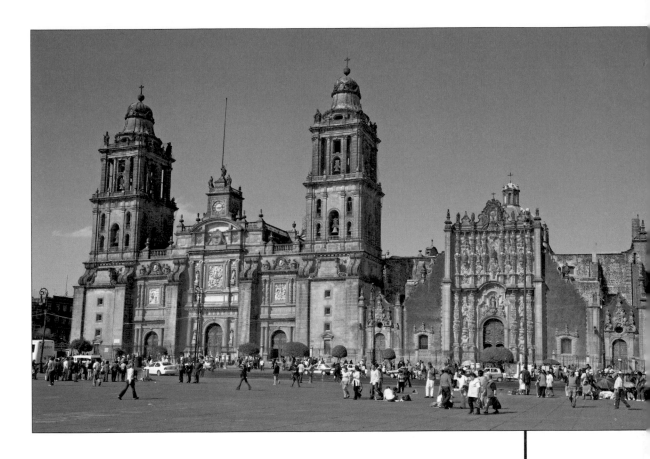

ride horses. Everyone had to pay heavy taxes. The Spanish used force, even killing many who resisted them.

The people were very unhappy. They wanted to make changes. No one knew how to begin. They needed a leader to take charge and rally the people. Father Miguel Hidalgo became that person.

The Spanish built many cathedrals, such as the Metropolitan Cathedral in Mexico City. They took many years to build.

Father Miguel Hidalgo inspired the Mexicans to fight for independence, as shown in this painting.

MEXICAN INDEPENDENCE

*

IN 1753, A CATHOLIC PRIEST WAS BORN IN A small town one hundred miles north of Mexico City. Mexico City was the capital of New Spain. Father Miguel Hidalgo (me-gal hi-DAHL-go) was well liked and a good speaker.

Miguel's parents were Spanish. His father was in charge of a large estate or hacienda (hah-see-EN-dah). Miguel was the youngest of four boys. He was a very good student and he studied hard.

After graduating with honors, he became a priest. He taught at a college for many years. Father Hidalgo read many kinds of books. He read about freedom and democracy. He believed that all of the people of Mexico should be free to govern themselves. He thought the Spanish rulers were wrong to treat the Mexican natives so badly. His ideas got him into trouble. He was removed from his teaching job.

In 1803, Hidalgo was sent to the small town of Dolores. There he served as a

This drawing shows Mexico City in the 1600s.

parish priest. The Native Mexicans of Dolores were very poor. They were forced to work long hours in the silver mines. The work was dangerous. Many times the walls of the mines caved in, and the miners were killed.

Other people worked in workshops or in the fields of the large haciendas. They had little food to eat. Their homes were small and crowded. What little money they earned went to the landowners to pay rent.

Father Hidalgo wanted to make life better for the Mexican people. He tried to help them set up small businesses. Some wove cloth. Others made wine or raised bees for honey. The Spanish rulers closed the businesses down.

Today, Mexico City is much bigger and busier!

Father Hidalgo used his home as a schoolroom. He taught many Mexicans to read and write. He tried to get employers to treat the people better. However, Father Hidalgo could not change the thinking of the Spanish rulers.

The only way there could be changes was to overthrow, or get rid of, the Spanish government in Mexico. On September 16, 1810, Father Hidalgo began ringing church bells. The people heard the bells. They left the mines and fields and came to the church.

Father Hidalgo shouted to the people to rise up against the Spanish rulers.

No one wrote down Father Hidalgo's exact words. People remember some of what he said. "Long live our Lady of Guadalupe! Down with bad government! Death to all Spaniards!" The Lady of Guadalupe was another name for the Virgin Mary, the mother of Jesus. Mexican natives honored the Virgin

Mary. They believed she appeared to Juan Diego, a poor Indian, in the 1500s.

Father Hidalgo's cries for freedom were called the Grito de Dolores (GREE-to day do-lor-ays), or the Cry of Dolores. The Mexicans were moved by Father Hidalgo's words. They grabbed picks, shovels, pitchforks, and other tools to use as weapons. They made banners with pictures of the Virgin Mary on them. Carrying the banners, they began to march through the streets in Dolores. They were ready to fight for their freedom from the Spanish rulers.

First they attacked the silver mine. Then they charged a stone fortress. When the fortress was destroyed, the people began to attack the haciendas. The Spanish soldiers were outnumbered by the huge crowd of Mexicans.

Mexicans may have carried banners like this one while they fought against the Spanish.

As the people marched, more and more Mexicans joined the fight. In a few weeks, more than eighty thousand people had joined with Father Hidalgo. They no longer feared the Spanish.

However, the Spanish troops were very strong. After a few small victories, Father Hidalgo's followers were defeated. A year later, in 1811, Father Hidalgo was captured and put to death. Still, the Mexican people would not give up. Father Hidalgo had given them hope. They continued to fight for their freedom. It took ten more years. Finally, in 1821, Mexico won its independence from Spain.

Each year on September 16, Mexican people everywhere remember Father Hidalgo. He is called the Father of Mexican Independence. Church bells ring in honor of this man. People repeat his famous speech, the Grito de Dolores.

Cities with large numbers of Mexican Americans have many activities to celebrate Mexican Independence Day.

Many places celebrate
Mexican Independence Day
with parades and festivals.

Parades are popular in California, Arizona, and Texas. Thousands of people line the streets to watch. Mexican-American community groups march down the street. There are marching bands. Famous Mexican Americans from sports, entertainment, and politics ride in cars and wave to the crowds.

Some people carry the Mexican flag. The flag has three large stripes: green, white, and red. Each color stands for a different idea. Green stands for independence. White stands for religious freedom. Red stands for unity. In the center of the flag is an eagle. The bird stands on a prickly pear cactus plant. In its mouth is a snake. According to a legend, the Aztecs saw an eagle eating a snake. They built their capital on that spot. Later, Mexico City was built in the same place as the Aztec capital.

Each part of the Mexican flag has a special meaning.

On Mexican Independence Day, people like to watch folk dances. Dance is an important part of Mexican culture. Culture is the way people dress, what they eat, the music they play, their beliefs, and their customs.

The dancers wear colorful costumes. The women wear brightly colored long, full skirts with ruffles. The skirts swish and swirl as the women dance. Male dancers wear a rodeo-rider costume called a charro (CHAR-ro). Some men wear sombreros. Dancers twirl and stamp their feet to the beat of the music. Some of the dances are very old. Many of them are based on ancient American Indian stories.

Some dancers dress in traditional Aztec costumes with lots of feathers. The dances tell about gods and emperors. Dances help Mexican Americans remember their Mexican heritage.

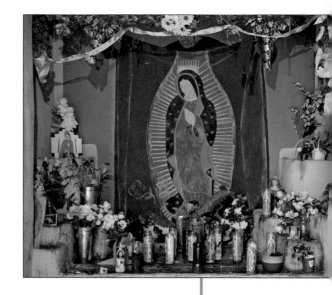

Many people have small areas in their houses or neighborhoods dedicated to Our Lady of Guadalupe.

Delicious foods such as tacos, guacamole, and refried beans are an important part of Mexican celebrations.

The Mexican hat dance, called jarabe tapatio (hah-RA-bay ta-pa-TEE-yo), is the national dance of Mexico. The dancers take quick hopping steps around a sombrero that is placed on the floor.

Carnivals, street fairs, and celebrations held in parks are the other ways Mexican Americans celebrate Independence Day.

Green, white, and red balloons decorate booths. Paper flowers made from tissue paper are tied to fences and poles.

Everywhere there are the smells of delicious Mexican food. Some people sell tacos, burritos, enchiladas, rice, beans and menudo (may-NOO-do). Menudo is a soup or stew. Many families bring their own food and have a picnic. In the evening, fireworks often burst across the sky. Everyone remembers the brave men and women who struggled for Mexican freedom.

BENITO JUAREZ

AFTER MEXICO GAINED INDEPENDENCE IN 1821, the country needed new laws. A new government had to be formed. This was not easy to do. The Mexican people had very little experience. Spain had controlled everything.

Native Mexican soldiers, who had fought against the Spanish, were the first ones to control the government. Then other groups tried to take control. For forty years, control of the government shifted back and forth between different groups. Civil wars broke

This is a painting of the Battle of Buena Vista, fought on February 23, 1847. The American army (right) was victorious.

out between the two main groups. The government was weak. During this time of weakness, United States and Mexican troops clashed in a border dispute. On May 12, 1846, the United States declared war on Mexico. Two years later, the war ended with Mexico's surrender. As a result, Mexico lost its territories in the United States. This land became the states of California, Nevada, Utah, Arizona, and New Mexico.

Benito Juarez (be-NEE-to hoo-AR-ays) was a Zapoteca Indian. He was born in 1806. His parents were poor peasants. Both of them died when Benito was three years old. He was raised by grandparents and later an uncle.

At age thirteen, Benito moved to the city of Oaxaca (wah-HA-kah). He worked for a man who was a bookbinder. Benito could not read or write. His employer liked Benito and adopted him. He helped the boy learn to read and write. Benito studied very hard.

When he grew up, Juarez became a lawyer. He was very smart and honest. The government tried to take away land that belonged to Mexican natives. Juarez helped the people protect their land. He defended poor people in court. In 1841, Juarez became a judge. Six years later, he was elected governor of the state of Oaxaca.

Many people hoped that Benito would make Mexico strong and peaceful.

Many memorials have been built to honor Benito Juarez and tell visitors about this great president of Mexico.

While governor, he built roads and schools. Everyone knew about his honesty.

Meanwhile, the civil wars between government groups were still going on. People were tired of the fighting and killing. Many people thought that Juarez might be able to make the country stronger. They hoped he could bring about peace and unity. In 1860, the people elected Benito Juarez president of Mexico.

BATTLE OF PUEBLA

PRESIDENT JUAREZ HAD A BIG PROBLEM. THE Mexican government owed a lot of money to other countries. One of the countries was France. If Juarez paid the money, there would be nothing left in the treasury to help Mexicans. He chose to use the money to help his people.

This angered Napoleon III (Louis Napoleon), the ruler of France. Napoleon III

In 1861, Napoleon III sent troops to make Mexico a French colony.

invaded Mexico to make the country a French colony. Napoleon III's army was the strongest and best trained in Europe. In December of 1861, the French army attacked Veracruz (VAY-rah-croos), Mexico's largest port city. The people in Veracruz surrendered to the French.

Then the French began the 400 mile march to Mexico City. They planned to capture the capital and take control of the government. On May 4, the French army camped near a town called Puebla (poo-AY-blah). The small town was halfway between Veracruz and Mexico City.

The Mexican general, Ignacio Zaragoza (ig-NAH-see-o sah-rah-go-sah), tried to stop the French forces. Outside Puebla were two hills. Zaragoza placed most of his soldiers on the hills. General Zaragoza did not expect to win. Many of his men had been soldiers for less than three months. Others knew nothing

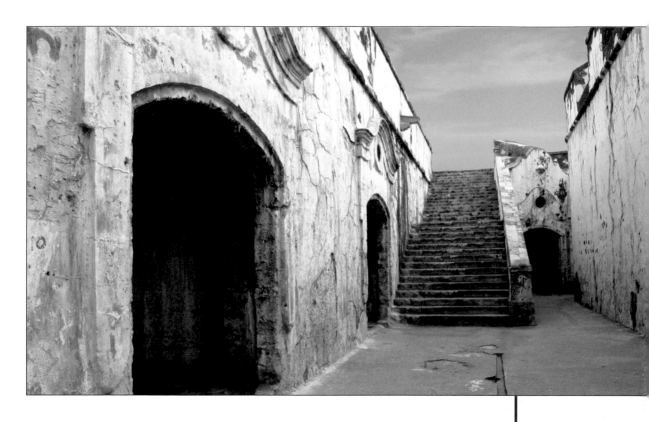

This is part of the fort at Veracruz that the French captured.

about fighting against well-trained soldiers. The Mexicans had crude weapons. Zaragoza only hoped to slow the French invasion. He wanted to give President Juarez more time to fortify the capital.

The French attacked on the morning of May 5, 1862. They stormed up the hills. Brave Mexicans fired muskets

Ignacio Zaragoza, a Mexican general, stopped the French army from capturing Mexico City.

In 1863, Napoleon III made Archduke Maximilian from Austria the emperor of Mexico.

(old-fashioned, long-barreled guns) and cannons. Many of the French soldiers were driven back down the hills. Then it began to rain. The slopes of the hills turned into mud. It became difficult for the French to advance. After four hours, the French gave up the battle. They withdrew back to Veracruz. The small ragged group of Mexican soldiers had defeated the powerful French army.

A year later, the French army tried again. This time, they succeeded. The French army captured Mexico City. Napoleon III made an Austrian archduke, Maximilian, the emperor of Mexico. For the next five years, the Mexican people fought the French. Benito Juarez led the fight. The victory at Puebla gave them courage and spurred them on.

If they could defeat the French once, they could beat them again. In 1867, the Mexican people succeeded. They overthrew Maximilian. Napoleon III removed all his troops from Mexico.

Once again Juarez became the leader of the country. He brought about reform and many changes. He is remembered as one of Mexico's greatest presidents.

This great president made Cinco de Mayo, which is Spanish for the fifth of May, a national holiday. He did not want people to forget the brave men who fought against the French. Every May 5, Mexican people remember the victory over the French at the Battle of Puebla.

After five years of fighting, the Mexicans overthrew the French. Benito Juarez was president again.

TIME TO CELEBRATE

MEXICAN AMERICANS LOVE PARTIES AND celebrations. They call them fiestas (fee-ES-tahs). Fiesta also means "feast day." A feast day to Mexican Americans means music, dancing, colorful clothes, and good food.

Some people make their own tortillas (tor-TEE-yas), which are flat, pancakelike bread made from corn or wheat. But most buy their tortillas at the store. Tortillas are eaten every day and fixed in many ways.

They can be wrapped around meat, cheese, beans and rice. Frying or baking tortillas in different ways will make tacos, enchiladas, or burritos. Cheese and sauce are put on top of many Mexican dishes. Every fiesta means eating many delicious traditional foods.

Tortillas are an important part of many Mexican foods.

Often mariachi (mar-ee-AH-chee) bands play at fiestas. The bands are a symbol of Mexico. The band groups generally have six to eight members. There are usually two men that play the violin. The others play the trumpet, guitar, and bass. They sing and play favorite folk songs and popular music. Some folk songs like "La Cucaracha" (lah coo-ca-RAH-chah), which means "the cockroach" in Spanish, have been sung for hundreds of years.

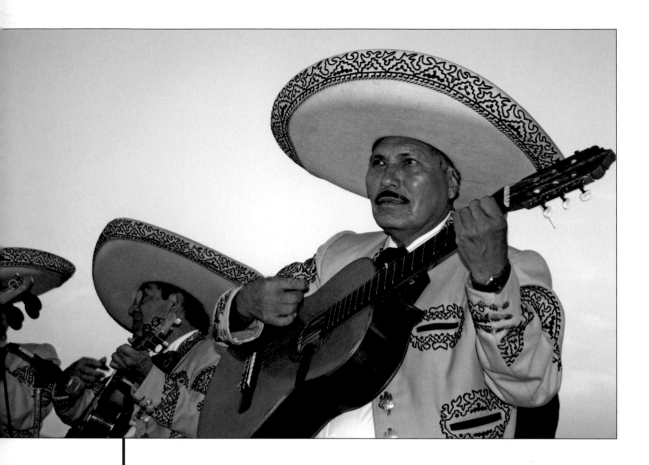

Mariachi bands play favorite folk songs at fiestas and other celebrations.

Mariachis dress in colorful costumes trimmed with silver buttons that flash in the sun. They often wear hats called sombreros.

Some people believe mariachis go back to when the French army occupied Mexico. Many French soldiers married Mexican women. They hired small bands

This family gets ready to participate in a Cinco de Mayo parade in Minnesota. They are wearing traditional Aztec dancing costumes.

Maracas are often part of the music in many Latin American countries.

to play at their weddings. The bands were later called mariachi because the French word for wedding is "marriage."

Whether this is true or not, everyone loves listening to the mariachis play. They are an important part of every celebration.

Many schools in the United States have special Cinco de Mayo celebrations. At a school in Orange, California, boys and girls put on a special Cinco de Mayo school fair. For weeks they plan for the big day. Some of the children learn Mexican songs and dances. Everyone helps make decorations for the school playground. Parents cook Mexican food. The excitement builds until the fiesta of Cinco de Mayo begins.

CINCO DE MAYO

ON CINCO DE MAYO, THE PLAYGROUND IS crowded with children and their families. Many boys and girls walk in a big circle while music plays. On the ground numbers are placed around the circle. Mexican music blares from the loudspeakers. Who will stop on the lucky number? The music stops. The walkers stop and look down at the numbers. Laughter and shouting greet the child who is standing on the winning number. The child wins a cake.

These girls are dancing at a Cinco de Mayo party in Alamogordo, New Mexico.

Over to the side, there are games like "lasso the bull." Each player has wooden rings. The rings are tossed at the horns of a paper bull. To win a prize, a ring must hang on the horn. Nearby are food booths. Children and their parents line up to buy tacos.

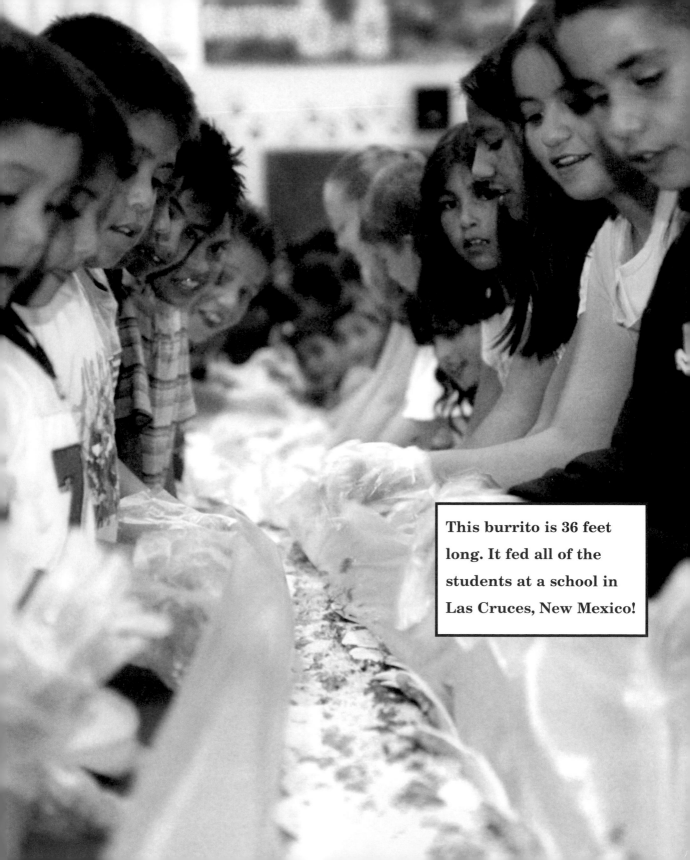

This burrito is 36 feet long. It fed all of the students at a school in Las Cruces, New Mexico!

Colorful tissue paper flowers are used as decorations during Cinco de Mayo celebrations.

Tree trunks and school fences are brightly decorated with tissue-paper flowers made by the boys and girls. Mexican-American children share their culture with one another. They enjoy telling other boys and girls about the Battle of Puebla.

Other Cinco de Mayo celebrations take place at parks and churches. There are many events: picnics with piñatas (peen-YAH-tas) for the children, puppet shows, baseball and soccer games, and carnivals. Museums have art shows. They display paintings and artwork created by Mexican Americans. Everywhere there are mariachis and folk dancers.

Many Mexican Americans look forward to celebrating Cinco de Mayo with their friends and neighbors. They enjoy eating Mexican food and going to fiestas. Cinco de Mayo has been celebrated in the United States

Piñatas, like this bull, are filled with candy. When it is broken, the candy falls to the ground for the children to collect.

People have lots of fun dressing up to celebrate Mexican Independence Day and Cinco de Mayo!

for more than one hundred years. Mexican Americans enjoy Cinco de Mayo. However, they consider their Independence Day to be the most important Mexican patriotic holiday.

Mexican Americans are proud of their history. Mexican Independence Day and Cinco de Mayo are important days to remember. Both holidays celebrate the courage of the Mexican people. They remind everyone that no matter how great the struggle, it is important to keep trying. Mexican Americans look forward to next year's Mexican Independence Day and Cinco de Mayo.

Olé (Oh-lay)!

bass—A large violinlike instrument that plays low notes.

charro—A rodeo-rider costume worn by male dancers.

colony—A territory that is far away from the country that rules it.

culture—The arts, beliefs, and customs that make up a way of life for a group of people.

custom—A tradition practiced by many generations of people.

fiesta—A Mexican celebration.

hacienda—A country estate owned by a rich Spanish landowner.

heritage—Traditions and beliefs passed down from earlier generations.

mariachi—A band of six to eight members that plays Mexican folk songs and popular music.

menudo—A type of soup or stew.

piñata—A hollow, treat-filled papier-mâché figure broken during Mexican celebrations.

pyramid—A huge stone structure that is square on the bottom and has four sides shaped like triangles.

sombrero—A wide-brimmed Mexican hat.

tortilla—A flat, pancakelike bread made from corn or wheat.

Further Reading

DeAngelis, Gina. *Mexico*. Mankato, Minn.: Blue Earth Books, 2003.

Nobleman, Marc Tyler. *Cinco de Mayo*. Minneapolis: Compass Point Books, 2005

Wade, Mary Dodson. *Cinco de Mayo*. New York: Children's Press, 2003

Internet Addresses

Cinco de Mayo
http://www.kiddyhouse.com/Holidays/Cinco/

Cinco de Mayo Activities
http://www.apples4theteacher.com/holidays/cinco-de-mayo/index.html#cincodemayoactivities

Mexico–Culture–Holidays
http://www.kidsculturecenter.com/mexico/mex_holiday.htm

INDEX